This book
belongs to:

....

....

My Friend Has Down Syndrome

Text: *Jennifer Moore-Mallinos*

Illustrations: *Marta Fàbrega*

Do you have a special friend?

I do! Her name is Tammy, and she's my best friend. I met Tammy last summer at camp, the kind you go to during the day but then return home to sleep. I've been going to that camp for as long as I can remember, but last summer was the best camp ever because that's when I met Tammy.

Last summer camp started out just like it did every year. The campers (that's what the kids were called), were divided into groups. There was a little kid group, a middle group, and a big kid group. I was in the middle group, because it was for kids who were seven, eight, or nine years old and I was eight.

Each group had a
camp leader. My camp
leader was Ms. Theresa. She was really
nice! Everyday she had something fun for us to
do; for example, we would go fishing off the dock
by the lake or swimming. Sometimes we played
beach volleyball or tag, and every Friday we did
arts and crafts. Also, last summer was the first
year that all the campers got to be in a talent show,
even the little kids!

 It was the end of the first week of camp when Ms. Theresa told us that there was going to be a new camper joining our group, and that her name was Tammy. Ms. Theresa said that she was going to need our help in making Tammy feel welcome and that she wanted one of us to be Tammy's buddy while she learned the ropes.

When Ms. Theresa asked me if I wanted to be Tammy's buddy I got excited! I was the most experienced camper in my group, so she thought that I was the best person for the job.

Ms. Theresa said that even though Tammy would spend most of her time with me, she expected all the campers to be patient and understanding, because Tammy had Down syndrome. That meant that she might need extra help with some of the activities we did, especially the talent show.

We all got a bit scared.
Probably because we didn't know much about Down syndrome. One kid was worried that we might all catch Down syndrome from Tammy and that maybe it wasn't a good idea that she would be with us. Then another kid wondered if Tammy should go to a special camp instead of ours, especially since she might need extra help.

Ms. Theresa said that our camp was
for all kids and that included Tammy.
Then she explained that a person with
Down syndrome is born with an extra gene.
When we asked what was that, she said that
all of us are born with genes, which are tiny
bits of matter inside our bodies, and genes
are what make us who we are.

Ms. Theresa said that kids with Down have features that make them look alike. They usually have flat faces and large, almond-shaped eyes, short arms and legs, small ears and a small mouth. Some kids with Down syndrome might have trouble hearing and seeing things, and some take longer to learn things. And did you know that some kids with Down syndrome grew up to be actors and actresses?

When the day came
for me to meet Tammy,
I was excited but also a bit
nervous. What if Tammy
didn't like me and didn't want
me to be her buddy? Mom told
me that I should just be myself and
let Tammy decide. So that's what
I did! And that's when
I knew that we'd become
friends, because no
matter what joke
I told, Tammy
always laughed!

Tammy was rather slow at some of the sports activities that we did, like running races and tag, but she was good at some other things. Tammy was really good at arts and crafts, especially pottery. She could take a blob of clay and mold it into anything, even pretty plates and vases! And when it was time to show our talents at the show I got very shy and wanted to quit, but Tammy made me feel brave and didn't let me give up.

Everybody loved our show! Tammy played the guitar and I played the tambourine and together we sang one of the songs we learned at camp. We were a great team! I even forgot about being ashamed! And the best part was that Tammy promised that she would teach me how to play the guitar.

Tammy and I have been friends ever since that first day when we met at camp and, like Tammy promised, she's teaching me how to play the guitar. Just like Tammy, I need help with some things too! And that's okay!

Parent Guide

The purpose of this book is to acknowledge the existence of Down syndrome among children and to eliminate existing barriers between these children and their peers. It also attempts to make readers aware that children diagnosed with Down syndrome have the potential and ability to become active participants among their peers and within society.

It is hoped that this book will promote a better understanding and acceptance of all children!

According to the National Down Syndrome Society, one out of 733 births and more than 350,000 people in the U.S. alone, have Down syndrome. Down syndrome is one of most recurring chromosomal abnormality among individuals.

Down syndrome is a genetic condition in which a person is born with an extra 21st chromosome, for a total of 47 chromosomes rather than 46. Although Down syndrome cannot be prevented, it can be detected during pregnancy.

This condition was discovered by Langdon Down in 1887; however, it was not until 1959 that the extra chromosome was detected.

Children with Down syndrome share certain facial and physical features such as a flat facial profile, an upward slant to the eyes, an enlarged tongue and a single crease across the center of their palms. Although many children with Down syndrome grow at a slower rate, they are able to reach developmental milestones. Many children with Down syndrome are often shorter than their peers of similar age.

Cognitive development often varies among individuals; however, most have mild to moderate impairments. Children may have delays in speech, fine and gross motor skills and may mature at a slower pace in regard to their emotional, social, and intellectual development.

Although goals are reached at a different pace for children with Down syndrome, many are capable of learning enough to become active members in society.

Some children may experience congenital heart defects, as well as hearing and visual deficits. These audio and visual deficits often affect a child's language and learning skills.

More frequent health conditions that occur in children with Down syndrome include thyroid problems, intestinal abnormalities, respiratory problems, obesity, an increased vulnerability to infections, and a higher risk of childhood leukemia. Some children may also experience seizures.

Individuals with Down syndrome have become accepted members of our society. Many opportunities are available for them to achieve their full potential. Recreational, educational, and social programs give individuals the chance to develop their skills and abilities, while providing them with the opportunity to discover hidden talents.

Many programs, including those adopted by the education system, have an integrated approach with respect to children with Down syndrome. Although mainstreaming is based on a child's academic and social abilities, most programs are of the full-inclusion kind.

Parents who first learn that their child has Down syndrome will often experience a range of emotions. Finding the appropriate information and support networks available within your community is helpful in alleviating many of these initial concerns.

There are many intervention programs available for your child, and some of these should match your child's individual needs. Some children may require physical, speech, and occupational assistance as well as specialized educational programs.

Many children with Down syndrome are active members in our society. Many individuals graduate from high school and many go on to complete college level education. Many individuals are able to find employment and live independently.

All children deserve a chance to reach their full potential and to develop lasting relationships. Perhaps by breaking down some of the barriers that exist between all children, every child, no matter what, will strive for excellence and become the best that he or she can be!

MY FRIEND HAS DOWN SYNDROME

First edition for the United States and Canada published
in 2008 by Barron's Educational Series, Inc.

© Copyright 2008 by Gemser Publications S.L.
El castell, 38; Teià (08329) Barcelona, Spain (World Rights)

Title of the original in Spanish: *Mi amiga tiene el síndrome
de Down*

Text: Jennifer Moore-Mallinos
Illustrations: Marta Fàbrega

All inquiries should be addressed to:
Barron's Educational Series, Inc.
250 Wireless Boulevard
Hauppauge, NY 11788
www.barronseduc.com

ISBN-13: 978-0-7641-4076-1
ISBN-10: 0-7641-4076-0

Library of Congress Control Number: 2008926682

Printed in China
9 8 7 6 5 4 3 2 1